Tapas

Delicious & Authentic Recipes

susaeta

Contents

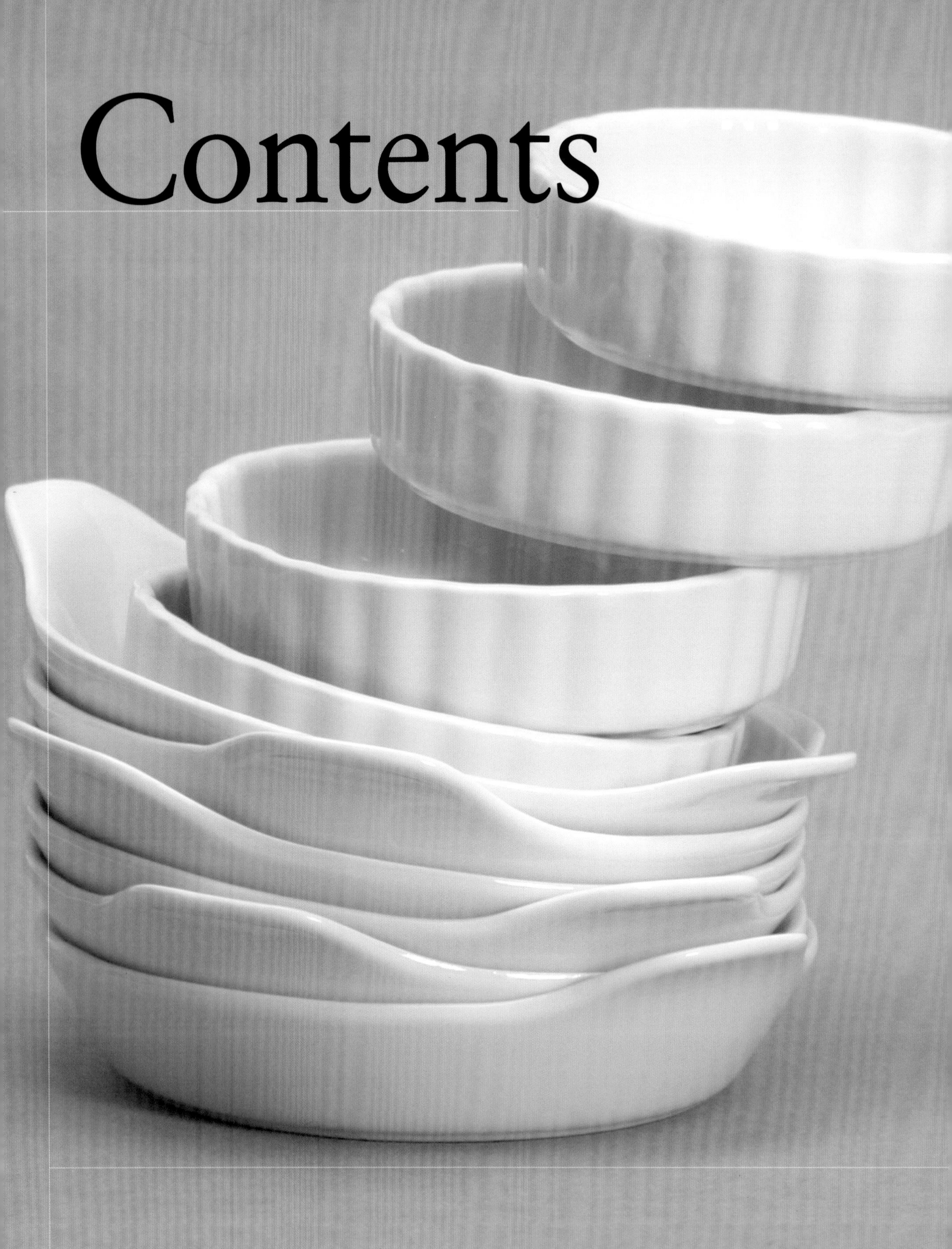

In Between Meals, *Tapas*

The custom of having tapas *is a fundamental part of Spanish life which has been exported to many countries.*

*Way back in the 13th century, following an illness which made him eat in between meals, King Alfonso X seriously advised tavern keepers to serve their jugs of wine covered with a slice of ham or cheese (*tapa *literally meaning "lid" or "cover" in Spanish) to prevent impurities from falling into the drink at the same time as it meant his subjects would avoid drinking on an empty stomach. This is the origin of* tapas *understood in this sense of the word, referring to an ancient custom today more alive than ever.*

As we have already mentioned, tapas *have traditionally been served with wine, usually the typical wine of the region:* chacolí *in the Basque Country; sherry in the South;* Penedès *in Catalonia;* Rioja *in Castile and* Ribeiro *in the North-west.*

Having tapas *is more or less a ritual for many; an important part of socialising for friends and colleagues who nibble away at all kinds of* tapas *whilst standing at the bar drinking wine.*

Garnishing Tips

STEP-BY-STEP

There are many varied ways to give your dishes that special finishing touch, which are easier than what you may think, especially if you use the right utensils.

Not only can tomatoes be scalded in order to remove the skin more easily, but can also be cut into various shapes, for example, that of an attractive flower, as shown below.

Turnovers always come in handy and are a tasty bite to eat. If you keep ready-made special dough in the fridge, turnovers can be rapidly improvised at any time, admitting a wide range of fillings available in any pantry.

Contrary to what many people think, croquettes are not so tedious to make. Just follow our step-by-step directions and you'll see there's no need to get your fingers sticky. Besides, our method is also more hygienic, using a forcing bag.

Tomato Flower

1. Choose a hard tomato, not too ripe. Rinse, dab dry well and, with a sharp knife, mark 6 triangles on the skin by just cutting the surface slightly.

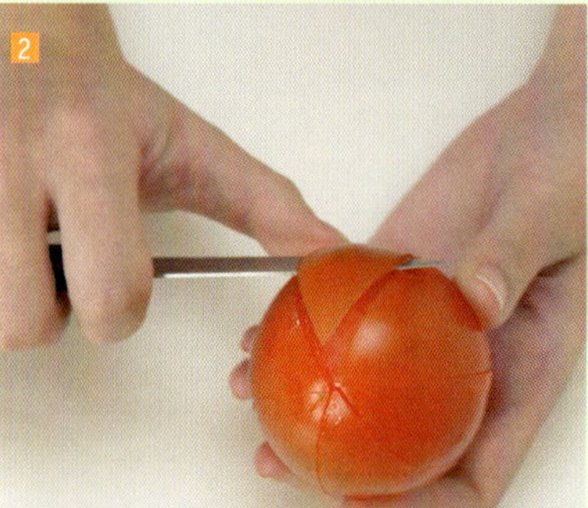

2. Peel the triangles halfway back, being careful not to touch the pulp.

3. Arrange the triangles into 6 petals.

Turnovers (Empanadillas)

1. Remove the special pastry rounds for making turnovers from the greaseproof paper separating them.
2. Put a little filling (e.g. tuna fish, onion and tomato) into the middle of each round.
3. Fold the pastry over, dampen the edges and press them together firmly with a fork.
4. Deep-fry in hot oil.

Croquettes

1. Prepare the croquette dough. When cold, turn it into a forcing bag. Fill a tray with breadcrumbs and pipe out the croquette dough.
2. Cut the dough into equal-sized croquettes.
3. Beat 1 egg, 1 tablespoonful of flour and 3 tablespoonfuls of water in a bowl. Coat each croquette in this batter and then in breadcrumbs. Deep-fry in hot oil.

Potato *Tapas*

Herb Potatoes

4 large potatoes

40 g basil

40 g rosemary

40 g chives

40 g leek

200 g butter

1 dl white wine vinegar

Salt

METHOD FOR 4 PORTIONS

1. Choose large potatoes in order to make as many balls as possible. Peel and rinse.
2. With a special scoop, make as many balls as you can. Put the balls in a pan with cold water and salt.
3. Bring to the boil. Simmer for a few minutes until cooked, taking care they aren't too soft. Remove from heat. Drain and set to one side.
4. Finely chop the basil, rosemary, leek and chives.
5. Prepare the sauce by carefully melting the butter in a pan, mixing in the vinegar and the white wine. Add the previously chopped herbs. Stir very well. Season to taste.
6. Place the potato balls on a serving dish and pour the herb dressing over.

Herb Potatoes

Garlic Potatoes

(Patatas alioli)

4 medium-sized potatoes

1 clove of garlic

Chopped parsley

Mayonnaise:

1 egg

3 dl olive oil

Juice of 1 lemon

Salt

METHOD FOR 4 PORTIONS

1. Choose special potatoes for boiling. Rinse well, but don't peel.
2. Fill a pan with cold water. Put the potatoes in and bring to the boil. Cook until ready.
3. Drain and set aside to cool. When cold, peel, dice and salt. Put them on a plate.
4. Meanwhile, peel the garlic and set to one side.
5. To make the mayonnaise, break 1 egg into a bowl. Add a little salt and, gradually, the oil, beating gently all the time. When the mixture thickens, add the lemon juice.
6. When the mayonnaise is ready, add the clove of garlic and mix in well.
7. Mix the potatoes with some of the garlic mayonnaise *(alioli)* and set the rest to one side.
8. Chop the parsley finely.
9. Last of all, place the potatoes on a serving dish. Pour over the rest of the *alioli* sauce. Sprinkle with the parsley.

Patatas alioli

Potatoes

with Mustard Dressing

1 kg potatoes

Mustard Dressing:

1 egg

salt

3 dl olive oil

5 tablesp. vinegar

1 glass of red wine (preferably Cariñena)

1/2 teasp. mustard

METHOD FOR 4 PORTIONS

1. Peel, rinse and cut potatoes into large cubes.
2. Put the potatoes in a pan with salted boiling water and cook for 5 minutes.
3. Drain well and put them into an oven dish. Sprinkle with almost all the wine (leave a little for the mayonnaise).
4. Cover the oven dish and place in a moderate preheated oven. Cook for 8 minutes, taking care that the potatoes do not break.
5. Separate the egg yolk from the white. Put the yolk in a bowl (and the white on a plate). Add a little salt and a few drops of vinegar. Beat well whilst gradually mixing in the oil. When the mayonnaise thickens, add the rest of the vinegar, the mustard and the rest of the wine.
6. Whisk the egg white until stiff. Add it to the mayonnaise. Mix well.
7. Pour the sauce over the potatoes and serve.

$1/2$ kg potatoes

$1/2$ onion

Olive oil

Vinegar

Parsley

Salt

Fried Potatoes with Onion

(Patatas a lo pobre)

METHOD FOR 4 PORTIONS

1. Choose medium-sized potatoes. Peel, rinse and cut into 0,5 cm rounds.
2. Peel and slice the onion.
3. Rinse and finely chop a sprig of parsley.
4. Heat oil in a pan and fry the potato rounds and onion over a low heat until the onion is soft. Stir occasionally, taking care not to break the potatoes and making sure the onion doesn't burn. When nearly ready, turn up the heat and brown the potatoes.
5. Remove pan from heat and turn onto a plate with kitchen paper to drain excess oil.
6. Place on a dish, season, sprinkle with vinegar and parsley.
7. Serve hot as an appetizer or to garnish meat or fish dishes.

Summer Salad

1 kg potatoes
2 eggs
1 green pepper
1 sprig of parsley
3 tomatoes
1 onion
5 tablesp. oil
1 clove of garlic
Salt
Pepper
3 tablesp. vinegar

METHOD FOR 4 PORTIONS

1 Choose special potatoes for boiling. Rinse well and put in a pan with cold water and a little salt. Cook for 20 minutes.

2 Once cooked, drain the potatoes. Set aside to cool a little. Peel, cut into thick slices and place them on a serving dish. Set to one side.

3 Wash the pepper, deseed and cut it very finely. Mix with the potatoes and set to one side.

4 Wash and finely chop the parsley.

5 Wash and slice the tomatoes, and arrange them around the potatoes and pepper.

6 Peel and finely chop the onion. Do the same with the clove of garlic.

7 Hard boil the eggs. Remove from heat and drain. Leave to cool for a few minutes under the tap and remove shells. Cut into wedges and arrange on top of the potatoes.

8 In a bowl, mix the vinegar, the onion, the parsley, the garlic, the salt and the pepper, stirring and gradually adding the oil. Pour the sauce over the potatoes, tomatoes, pepper and eggs.

9 Mix well and serve the salad chilled.

Summer Salad

Chorizo-Filled Potato Balls

1 kg potatoes

1 tablesp. butter

100 g chorizo sausage

Olive oil

Flour

METHOD FOR 4 PORTIONS

1. Choose special potatoes for boiling. Peel and rinse. Put in a pan with plenty cold water and cook until ready.
2. Once cooked, drain well and place in an ovenproof dish. Put in the oven for a few minutes.
3. Remove the potatoes from the oven. Mash well.
4. Separate the yolk from the white. Leave the egg white on a plate.
5. Add the egg yolk to the mashed potatoes, along with the previously softened butter and a little salt. Mix very well.
6. Cut the chorizo sausage into slices not too thick and remove the skin. Coat your hands in flour. Take a little mashed potato with a spoon. Put a slice of chorizo in the middle and cover it completely with more potato, shaping into a ball.
7. Beat the egg white and coat the potato balls.
8. Deep-fry the balls in very hot oil until golden.

Chorizo-Filled Potato Balls

Potato, Vegetable & Tuna Salad

(Ensaladilla rusa)

$1/2$ kg potatoes

$1/2$ kg carrots

$1/2$ kg runner beans

$1/2$ kg peas

1 egg

2 cans of tuna fish in oil

Salt

Sweet red pepper

Mayonnaise:

1 egg

3 dl olive oil

Salt

Juice of $1/2$ lemon

METHOD FOR 4 PORTIONS

1. Rinse the potatoes well.
2. Put the potatoes (without peeling) in a pan of cold water and a little salt. Cook until they are ready, but not too soft. To check cooking point, insert a skewer/fork. If it goes in easily and comes out clean, they are ready. Remove from heat and leave to cool. Peel and dice finely.
3. Wash the carrots and cook in the same way as the potatoes. Dice finely.
4. Repeat the same procedure with the rest of the vegetables, always cooking them separately.
5. Hard boil an egg. Cool it under the tap and set aside.
6. Make a thick mayonnaise by beating the egg, the oil and the salt. Add the lemon juice to flavour and thin the mayonnaise.
7. Put all the vegetables in a large bowl with the drained tuna. Gradually add the mayonnaise, mixing it well with all the vegetables. Keep a little mayonnaise for garnishing.
8. Turn the salad onto a dish or use special individual moulds to shape. Garnish with the remaining mayonnaise, the hard boiled egg and the sweet pepper.

1 kg potatoes

2 onions

50 g bacon

200 g mince

50 g breadcrumbs

1 egg

Salt

Pepper

Parsley

Juice of 1/2 lemon

5 tablesp. olive oil

1 small glass of white wine

1 dl water

2 tablesp. flour

1 clove of garlic

Potatoes Filled with Meatballs

METHOD FOR 4 PORTIONS

1 Choose large, elongated potatoes. Peel, rinse and cut the potatoes in half. Scoop out the centre.

2 Peel 1 onion. Chop it finely, together with the bacon.

3 Separate the egg yolk from the white.

4 Mix the mince, breadcrumbs, onion, bacon, egg yolk, salt, pepper, parsley and lemon juice in a bowl.

5 With this mixture, make meatballs the size of the space left by scooping out the potato. Put one meatball in each cavity. Brush with the beaten egg white and coat each potato half with flour and fry in hot oil. Remove from the pan and place in an oven dish (filled side facing up).

6 Using the same oil used to fry the potatoes, sauté the other onion (peeled and chopped) and the clove of garlic. Add 1 tablesp. flour, 1 dl water, the white wine and bring to the boil.

7 Pour this sauce over the potatoes and cook in a preheated oven at 150°C for about 20 minutes (or until ready). If necessary, add a little hot water.

Potato Omelette

(Tortilla de patata)

1 kg potatoes

1 onion

5 eggs

Olive oil

Salt

METHOD FOR 4 PORTIONS

1. Peel the potatoes, wash and finely slice.
2. Peel the onion and chop it finely.
3. Heat the oil in a frying pan and add the onion.
4. When the onion starts frying, add the potatoes and salt. Fry until soft (but not brown), stirring from time to time.
5. Remove pan from heat. Drain off as much oil as possible and set to one side.
6. Beat the eggs in a bowl with a pinch of salt.
7. Add the potatoes and the onion (well-drained) and mix until they soak up the egg.
8. Heat a little oil (just enough to coat the pan bottom) in a non stick frying pan.
9. Make the omelette over a low heat. When set on the bottom, turn the omelette, with the help of a plate. When ready, turn onto a plate.
10. Serve cut in cubes or triangles.

Tortilla de patata

Potatoes

with Spinach

4 medium-sized potatoes

300 g spinach

4 tablesp. grated cheese

2 tablesp. breadcrumbs

1 tablesp. sesame seeds

2 tablesp. olive oil

Salt

METHOD FOR 4 PORTIONS

1. Choose special potatoes for boiling. Fill a pan with cold water and a little salt. Add the potatoes (whole) and bring to the boil. Cook until nearly soft, pricking with a fork. Remove pan from heat.
2. Drain, peel and cut into rounds. Put the potato rounds on a plate. Set to one side.
3. If the spinach is fresh, rinse well several times, changing water. When clean, chop finely.
4. Put the spinach in a pan and cover with water and a pinch of salt. Bring to the boil and cook for approximately 10 to 15 minutes. Drain very well to get rid of any excess water. Heat a little oil in a frying pan and sauté the spinach.
5. In a bowl, mix the cheese, bread and the sesame seeds.
6. Take an ovenproof dish. Arrange some potato rounds on the bottom of the dish. Top each potato round with a little spinach. Repeat the process as necessary. Top everything with the cheese mixture.
7. Preheat the oven at 275°C. Place dish in oven and grill for a few minutes.

Potatoes with Spinach

Meat *Tapas*

Stewed Beef

1 kg lean beef

1 onion

2 carrots

2 leeks

1 tablesp. parsley

5 tablesp. olive oil

1 glass of white wine

1 glass of water

Salt

Pepper

METHOD FOR 4 PORTIONS

1. Remove any fat from the meat and dice it.
2. Peel and finely chop the cloves of garlic and the onion.
3. Wash, peel and dice the carrots.
4. Rinse the leeks to get rid of any soil. Cut off the green part and chop finely.
5. Wash the parsley and chop it finely.
6. Heat the oil in a large frying pan. Add the onion, the parsley, the leeks and the garlic. Sauté. Season the meat and add the vegetables. Stir continuously so that the ingredients don't stick. Fry until golden.
7. Once the meat is brown, add the wine and water and cook over a low heat for approximately 1 hour until the meat is tender. If necessary, more water may be added (in small quantities).
8. To check if the meat is ready, prick with a fork or skewer. If it goes in easily it will be ready.
9. The meat may be served with the vegetables whole or with the sauce strained and then poured over the meat.

Stewed Beef

Stewed Kidneys

700 g calf's kidneys

2 tablesp. olive oil

1 small glass of sherry

1 small glass of stock

1 teasp. flour

25 g butter

Salt

White pepper

METHOD FOR 4 PORTIONS

1. Clean the kidneys carefully, discarding the skin and fat. Cut the kidneys horizontally into pieces and put them in a colander.
2. Fill a saucepan with water and bring to the boil. Lower the colander with the kidneys into the boiling water and scald for 1 minute. Remove from the pan. Dab dry with a clean cloth and season with salt and pepper.
3. Heat the oil in a frying pan. Sauté the kidneys over a high heat for 5 minutes. Set aside to drain in a colander.
4. Put the sautéed kidneys in a pan. Add the sherry and cook for exactly 2 minutes.
5. Melt the butter and stir in the flour. Mix in the stock gradually making sure there are no lumps. Simmer for a few minutes. Season with salt and pepper. Pour the sauce over the kidneys leaving them on the heat but without cooking any more.
6. Serve immediately. Don't allow to get cold.

Stewed Kidneys

Lamb's Sweetbread

with Ham

1 kg lamb's sweetbread

200 g Iberian cured ham

Olive oil

1 kg potatoes

2 tablesp. butter

1 litre of milk

Salt

METHOD FOR 4 PORTIONS

1. Clean the sweetbread well discarding the skin and fat. Put in cold water and leave for 3 hours.
2. Drain well. Dab dry with a cloth and chop into more or less equal-sized pieces.
3. Heat oil in a frying pan. Sauté the sweetbread until golden. Remove from the pan and drain on kitchen paper or a napkin.
4. Next, in the same oil used for frying the sweetbread, sauté the ham cut in medium-sized slices.
5. In a bowl, mix the sweetbread with the ham. Keep warm.
6. Peel, wash and cut the potatoes. Cook in salted boiling water for about 30 minutes or until the potatoes are cooked.
7. Drain the potatoes and mash. Put the mashed potatoes into a bowl and mix with the butter.
8. Heat the milk in a pan. When it boils, remove pan from the fire. Pour the milk into the mashed potatoes.
9. Season according to taste. Mix well, making sure there are no lumps.
10. Serve the mashed potatoes on a plate with the sweetbread and ham on top.

- 1 $1/2$ kg calf's tripe
- $1/2$ kg chick-peas
- 150 g chorizo sausage
- 1 ham bone
- 1 onion
- 2 tomatoes
- 3 tablesp. olive oil
- Vinegar
- 1 lemon
- Salt
- Grains of black pepper
- 1 tablesp. paprika
- 1 bay leaf
- Sprig of mint

Stewed Chick-Peas & Tripe

METHOD FOR 4 PORTIONS

1. Soak the chick-peas in water the evening before.
2. Clean the tripe carefully, scraping with a knife and chop into small pieces. Put the tripe in a bowl and change the water several times. Drain and add vinegar, salt and some lemon wedges. Rub the tripe until white. Rinse again several times until it is completely clean.
3. Peel and finely chop the onion. Set aside 1 tablespoonful of chopped onion.
4. Wash the tomato, scald for 2 minutes in boiling water. Peel, deseed and chop.
5. Heat the oil in a frying pan. Sauté the spoonful of onion along with the tomatoes.
6. Put the tripe in a saucepan. Cover with cold water and cook for 5 minutes. Drain well. Add cold water and bring to the boil. Add the chick-peas, the rest of the onion, the bay leaf, the mint, the paprika, the ham bone and salt. Simmer for 2 hours. Add the tomato sauce and the chorizo sausage. Check seasoning. Add a few grains of pepper. Cook for a further 2 hours until the tripe and chick-peas are tender.

Marinated Fillet of Pork

Fillet of pork for 4
3 cloves of garlic
1 teasp. oregano
4 tablesp. vinegar
1 teasp. sweet paprika
1 small glass of water
Olive oil
Salt

METHOD FOR 4 PORTIONS

1. It's best to marinate the pork the evening before to allow the flavours to develop.
2. Cut the meat into medium-sized pieces.
3. Peel the garlic and cut in half lengthwise.
4. In a deep bowl, prepare the marinade with the oregano, the garlic, 4 spoonfuls of vinegar, paprika, salt and a little water.
5. Add the meat to the marinade, making sure that it is all mixed together thoroughly. Leave in the refrigerator all night.
6. The next day, take the meat out of the bowl. Drain off any excess liquid.
7. Heat the oil in a frying pan and sauté the meat, removing the garlic so that it won't burn. Serve as a hot *tapa*.

Marinated Fillet of Pork

Liver & Onions

$^1/_2$ kg veal's liver or lamb's liver

2 onions

$^1/_2$ kg tomatoes

25 g pine nuts

50 g fat bacon

50 g lard

1 small glass of white wine

2 cloves of garlic

Salt

Pepper

METHOD FOR 4 PORTIONS

1. Chop the bacon into small pieces.
2. Melt the lard in a pan. Add the bacon and sauté until golden.
3. Chop the onion finely and add it with the liver chopped in small pieces.
4. Peel and dice the tomatoes. Scald for 2 minutes in boiling water so that the skin will come off easier.
5. After a few minutes, add the tomatoes and the wine. Season and cover. Cook for 1 hour over a low heat.
6. Crush the pine nuts and the garlic. Add a little water. Add this mixture to the liver when it is half cooked.
7. The stewed liver and onions may be garnished with slices of bread fried in oil or sprinkled with pine nuts, whichever you prefer.

Liver & Onions

Fried Veal, Ham & Cheese Rolls

(Flamenquines)

4 thin veal fillets

8 slices of cheese

4 slices cured ham

3 eggs

8 tablesp. flour

8 tablesp. breadcrumbs

Freshly-ground black pepper

Olive oil

METHOD FOR 4 PORTIONS

1. Put 2 eggs in a small pan. Cover with water and hard boil (10 minutes). Remove from heat and cool under a cold tap. Peel and chop finely.
2. Season the fillets with pepper. Cover each fillet with 2 slices of cheese. Put a slice of cured ham on the cheese. On top of the ham, put a little chopped egg.
3. Roll the fillets up and tie well with butcher's string or fasten with cocktail sticks.
4. Put the flour on one plate and the breadcrumbs on another. Beat the remaining egg on a deep plate.
5. Coat each roll in flour, egg and then breadcrumbs.
6. Heat the oil in a deep frying pan. Fry each *flamenquín* until golden. Put on a plate with kitchen paper to drain off any excess oil.
7. Serve hot.

1 kg pig's ear
1 bay leaf
2 onions
Unrefined salt
1 carrot
4 cloves of garlic
1 ripe tomato
A pinch of thyme
1 teasp. paprika
1 chilli pepper
4 tablesp. olive oil
Salt
Pepper

Stewed Pig's Ear

METHOD FOR 4 PORTIONS

1. Clean the ears carefully.
2. Put the ears into a pan with cold water, the bay leaf, 1 whole onion and the unrefined salt. Simmer for 2 to 3 hours until tender. Drain, but don't discard the cooking water.
3. Slice or dice the ears. Put to one side.
4. Peel and chop the other onion.
5. Rinse, peel and dice the carrot.
6. Peel and finely chop the garlic.
7. Scald the tomato for 2 minutes in boiling water to help remove the skin. Peel, deseed and chop.
8. Heat the oil in a pan and sauté the chopped onion, carrot and garlic for 5 minutes.
9. Add the tomato, a pinch of thyme, the paprika, the chilli pepper and 2 ladlefuls of the cooking water. Add the pig's ear and cook for a further 5 minutes.
10. Season and serve hot.

Marinated Chicken

1 chicken

75 g flour

250 ml chicken stock

5 tablesp. olive oil

Salt

Pepper

Marinade:

1/2 litre white wine

1 large onion

1 leek

1 carrot

1 stalk of celery

2 cloves of garlic

10 grains of pepper

METHOD FOR 4 PORTIONS

1. Clean the chicken, removing the fat. Chop into pieces not too big.
2. Prepare the marinade by washing, peeling and finely chopping all the vegetable ingredients.
3. Put the vegetables in a bowl along with the rest of the marinade ingredients. Add the chicken pieces. Cover and leave to marinate in the refrigerator for at least 1 day. Afterwards, drain the chicken, dab it dry with kitchen paper and coat in flour. Keep the juice and the vegetables from the marinade.
4. Heat oil in a pan and fry the chicken until golden. Add the marinated vegetables and sauté until brown.
5. Add the marinade juice. Season. When it starts to boil, turn down the heat and cook for 1 hour.
6. When the chicken is tender, put it on plates and keep warm.
7. Stir the sauce with a wooden spoon; allow it to evaporate a little until it thickens. Check seasoning and pour the sauce over the chicken when serving.

Marinated Chicken

Blood Pudding

with Tomato

$^1/_2$ kg blood pudding

1 onion

1 green pepper

2 cloves of garlic

1 kg ripe tomatoes

7 tablesp. olive oil

1 bay leaf

Salt

1 teasp. sugar

METHOD FOR 4 PORTIONS

1. Peel and chop the onion finely.
2. Wash the pepper, discard the seeds and cut into strips.
3. Peel and chop the garlic.
4. Heat 3 spoonfuls of oil in a pan and gently fry the above ingredients, taking care that they don't burn. Stir from time to time until ready. Remove from the pan and set to one side.
5. Scald the tomatoes for 2 minutes in boiling water to make them easier to remove their skin. Peel and dice.
6. Pour the rest of the oil into the same pan and fry the tomato. Cover the pan and cook over a low heat. Add the ingredients fried in step 4. Check seasoning and, if necessary, add a tablespoonful of sugar to reduce the tomato acidity.
7. Cut the blood pudding into equal-sized pieces. Add to the pan and stir carefully with a wooden spoon.
8. Cook for a few minutes with the bay leaf and serve warm.

Blood Pudding with Tomato

Fish/Shellfish *Tapas*

Pickled Mackerel Steaks

$1/2$ kg mackerel

1 onion

12 tablesp. olive oil

5 tablesp. vinegar

1 bay leaf

A pinch of thyme

Rosemary

2 cloves of garlic

Salt

METHOD FOR 4 PORTIONS

1. Clean the mackerel, cut into steaks, season with salt and flour lightly.
2. Heat some oil in a pan and fry the mackerel on both sides until slightly brown. Put to one side in another pan.
3. Peel and slice the onion. Peel the garlic.
4. Heat some oil in another pan and sauté the whole cloves of garlic, the sliced onion, the bay leaf, the thyme and the rosemary. Add the vinegar and a little salt.
5. When the onion is cooked, add it to the pan with the mackerel, making sure all the fish is covered.
6. Leave to cool for 2 hours. Serve at room temperature.
7. The mackerel can be eaten immediately or cold. It will keep in the refrigerator for up to five days. If kept in the fridge, take it out a little while before serving.

Pickled Mackerel

Tuna Pie

(Empanada gallega)

For the Filling:

1 onion

1 pepper

1 clove of garlic

1 sprig of parsley

2 cans of tuna fish in olive oil

2 tomatoes

Salt

Pepper

Sweet paprika

Olive oil

2 hard boiled eggs

For the Pastry:

250 g flour

5 dl water

5 dl milk

6 tablesp. oil

1/2 teasp. salt

1/2 teasp. sweet paprika

baker's yeast (1/2 walnut size)

METHOD FOR 4 PORTIONS

1. Prepare the filling. Heat the oil in a frying pan and sauté the onion, the pepper, the garlic and the parsley (all finely chopped).
2. When half cooked, season, add the tomato (peeled, deseeded and chopped). Cook until ready. Add a pinch of sweet paprika and the tuna fish. Cook a little more and then remove from the heat. Set aside to cool.
3. Make the pastry. Put the flour in a large bowl, make a hole in the centre and add the other ingredients. Mix well with a wooden spoon. Finish kneading with your hands on a flat surface until you get a smooth dough, without any lumps nor sticky (more flour may be added to prevent the dough from sticking).
4. Roll the dough into a ball and leave it to rest for approximately 1 hour. Afterwards, cut the dough in two, one half for the base and the other for the top. Roll out both parts with a rolling pin, forming two circles 2 mm thick.
5. Grease a round pastry tin, and line with 1 layer of the pastry dough. Pour in the filling (previously drained) and add the hard boiled eggs, sliced. Cover with the other part, pressing the edges well together so that the pie is sealed perfectly. If you wish, decorate with strips of pastry trimmings. Make a hole in the centre for the pie to breathe.
6. Brush all over with beaten egg and cut a few symmetrical slits with a scissor so that the filling will not break out during cooking.
7. Put the pie in a preheated oven at 200°C for 45 minutes until golden.

Empanada gallega

Prawn Cocktail

½ kg prawns

1 egg

1 teasp. mustard

Paprika

4 tablesp. olive oil

1 tablesp. lemon juice

1 tablesp. brandy

2 tablesp. single cream

3 tablesp. tomato ketchup

6 lettuce leaves

1 sprig of parsley

Worcester Sauce

Salt

METHOD FOR 4 PORTIONS

1. Put the prawns in a pan and cover with cold water. Cook for a few minutes. Remove from heat and drain well. Peel, discarding heads. Set to one side.
2. Wash the lettuce leaves and dry well. Chop finely. Put to one side.
3. Put 4 individual bowls into the refrigerator to chill.
4. Separate the egg yolk and white. Mix the yolk with the mustard and a pinch of paprika.
5. Mix well, stirring all the time whilst adding the oil gradually, taking care that the mayonnaise doesn't separate.
6. Add a tablespoonful of lemon juice, the ketchup, a dash of Worcester sauce, the brandy and the cream.
7. Mix well. Season according to taste.
8. Put the chopped lettuce into the chilled bowls. Add the prawns and cover with the mayonnaise.
9. Sprinkle with chopped parsley and serve immediately.

- 1 kg tuna fish
- 500 g tomatoes
- 2 onions
- 1 sprig of parsley
- 50 g walnuts
- 7 tablesp. olive oil
- 3 red peppers
- Salt
- Pepper

Tuna with Tomatoes, Peppers & Onions

METHOD FOR 4 PORTIONS

1. Take the central part of the fish. Remove skin, bones and fillet.
2. Wash and peel the tomatoes. (To make the skin easier to remove, scald the whole tomatoes in boiling water for a few minutes). Deseed and dice.
3. Wash, deseed and cut the peppers into strips.
4. Finely chop the onion, garlic, parsley (previously rinsed) and nuts. Set to one side.
5. Put a tablespoonful of oil into a heatproof dish. Put a layer of the previous mixture, and, on top, place tuna fish fillets. Repeat the process again. Top with the peppers.
6. Drizzle with the rest of the oil. Cook over a low heat until nearly ready. Place in the oven to finish cooking.
7. Garnish with the chopped nuts.

Pompano

with Tomatoes & Peppers

1 large pompano (mackerel)

75 g flour

1 onion

1 green pepper

4 tablesp. olive oil

½ kg ripe tomatoes

Salt

METHOD FOR 4 PORTIONS

1. Clean the fish discarding the skin. Fillet and cut into smaller chunks.
2. Salt the fish and coat it with flour.
3. Heat the oil in a pan. Fry the fish until slightly golden. Set aside on a plate. Keep this oil for later.
4. Peel and finely chop the onion.
5. Wash and deseed the pepper. Cut into strips.
6. To make it easier to peel the tomatoes, scald them for a couple of minutes in boiling water. Peel, deseed and crush the tomatoes.
7. In the same oil used for frying the fish, sauté the onion and the pepper until soft. Next add the crushed tomatoes and cook until the juice has evaporated a little.
8. Place the fish chunks on top of the tomato and pepper sauce. Cover the pan and simmer for 15 minutes.
9. Serve very hot.

Pompano with Tomatoes & Peppers

Mussels

in Vinaigrette

1 kg mussels

1 green pepper

½ onion

2 small tomatoes

6 tablesp. olive oil

2 tablesp. vinegar

Salt

Pepper

1 sprig of parsley

METHOD FOR 4 PORTIONS

1. Choose good quality mussels, making sure that they are all closed. With a knife, clean the mussels very well under a cold tap, scraping off any dirt stuck to the shell. Discard any that are open.
2. Steam cook, in a covered saucepan, until they open up completely. Drain well, discarding any that have not opened.
3. Wash and deseed the pepper. Dab dry with kitchen paper and dice finely.
4. Peel the onion and cut it in the same way as the pepper.
5. Wash the tomatoes and dice finely.
6. Put the pepper, tomatoes, onion, vinegar, salt and pepper into a bowl. Mix the oil in gradually until you get a fine vinaigrette sauce.
7. Remove the empty part of the shell from each mussel. Place the part of the shell with the mussel on a dish. Pour the vinaigrette dressing over. Garnish with parsley.

Mussels in Vinaigrette

Fried Squid

(Calamares a la romana)

$1/2$ kg squid

2 lemons

75 g flour

2 eggs

Olive oil

Salt

METHOD FOR 4 PORTIONS

1. Clean the squid well, removing the outer skin, the backbone and the ink sacs. Separate the fins and tentacles.
2. Chop into equal-sized rings. Cut the fins and tentacles into pieces. Place in a bowl.
3. Squeeze 1 lemon and sprinkle the squid with the juice. Add a little olive oil. Mix and leave to marinate for about 30 minutes.
4. Salt the squid pieces and coat with flour and beaten egg.
5. Heat plenty of oil in a pan and, when hot, fry the squid until golden.
6. Drain on kitchen paper. Serve immediately, garnished with lemon wedges.

1 kg fresh anchovies

1 red pepper

2 ripe tomatoes

1 onion

6 tablesp. olive oil

2 tablesp. vinegar

Olive oil for frying

75 g flour

Fresh Anchovies with Roasted Vegetables

(Boquerones)

METHOD FOR 4 PORTIONS

1. Wash the pepper, tomatoes and peel the onion.
2. Put all the vegetables in the oven. Drizzle with a little oil. Roast.
3. When roasted, peel and deseed the pepper and tomatoes. Chop finely, together with the onion.
4. In a bowl, mix the onion, tomatoes, pepper, vinegar, salt and pepper, adding oil gradually. Set to one side.
5. Wash and gut the anchovies. Drain. Coat with flour.
6. Heat oil in a pan and deep-fry the anchovies until golden, a few at a time so that the oil will not lose its temperature. Drain on kitchen paper.
7. Place the anchovies on a serving dish. Pour over the sauce. Serve.

Cod Fritters

(Soldaditos de Pavía)

500 g cured cod

160 g flour

14 tablesp. cold water

10 g yeast

2 tablesp. oil

Olive oil

Juice of 1 lemon

Parsley

METHOD FOR 4 PORTIONS

1. Choose the central part of the cod and leave it to soak the day before, changing the water several times.
2. Once desalted, cut into equal-sized pieces. Put the pieces into a bowl together with the lemon juice. Set to one side.
3. Put the flour in another bowl. Make a hole in the centre and add a pinch of salt, the yeast, two tablespoonfuls of oil and the cold water. Mix well, cover and leave in a warm place until the batter has increased in size.
4. Coat the cod pieces in the batter.
5. Deep-fry the cod in hot oil until golden, in small batches so that the oil doesn't lose its temperature.
6. Place the fried fish to drain on kitchen paper. Serve garnished with parsley.

Soldaditos de Pavía

Fried Sardines

1 kg large sardines

1 clove of garlic

75 g flour

2 eggs

Olive oil

Salt

1 lemon

METHOD FOR 4 PORTIONS

1. Choose very fresh, large sardines.
2. Clean the sardines removing bones, heads and guts. Drain.
3. Peel and chop the garlic very finely. Put the flour on a plate.
4. Beat the eggs on another plate or in a bowl. Add the chopped garlic and a pinch of salt.
5. Cut the sardines open. Coat in flour and then in beaten egg.
6. Heat the oil in a pan. Fry the sardines on both sides until golden, in small batches so that the oil doesn't lose its temperature.
7. Leave to drain on kitchen paper. Serve garnished with lemon wedges.

Fried Sardines

Miscellaneous *Tapas*

Crayfish in Spicy Sauce

½ kg live crayfish

1 kg ripe tomatoes

½ onion

5 cloves of garlic

2 chilli peppers

6 tablesp. olive oil

Salt

1 teasp. sugar

METHOD FOR 4 PORTIONS

1. Wash the crayfish and discard those that are not alive.
2. Peel and chop the onion finely. Peel the garlic and chop into not-too-small slices.
3. Heat 3 tablespoonfuls of oil in a pan. Sauté the onion until soft. Add the garlic and sauté until golden. Turn the heat up and toss in the crayfish. Sauté the crayfish together with the chilli peppers until reddish in colour. Set aside.
4. Remove from the heat. Drain the crayfish, the onion and the garlic. Keep the oil.
5. Scald the tomatoes in boiling water for 2 minutes so that they will be easier to peel. Crush.
6. Pour the rest of the oil into the pan and fry the tomatoes over a low heat for 15 minutes. Add a little sugar to balance the acidity and season according to taste.
7. Add the crayfish, the onion and the garlic to the tomato sauce. Cook for a further 15 minutes.
8. Check seasoning and serve very hot.

Crayfish in Spicy Sauce

Spinach & Potato Croquettes

250 g spinach

10 tablesp. breadcrumbs

10 tablesp. flour

10 tablesp. olive oil

½ onion

2 eggs

Salt

Mashed Potatoes:

1 kg potatoes

1 litre milk

2 tablesp. butter

10 tablesp. grated cheese

Salt

METHOD FOR 4 PORTIONS

1. Choose special potatoes for boiling.
2. Peel and rinse the potatoes. Put them in a pan with cold water and boil until soft.
3. Drain and mash the potatoes.
4. Add the hot milk and the butter. Mix in well and add the grated cheese. Set aside to cool.
5. Wash the spinach carefully. Chop and cook in a little water. Drain well.
6. Put 3 tablespoonfuls of oil into a frying pan. Sauté the onion (finely chopped). When the onion is soft, add the spinach and season.
7. In a bowl, mix the mashed potatoes with the spinach. Season according to taste.
8. Using two spoons, make balls with this mixture. Coat with flour, beaten egg and breadcrumbs.
9. Heat the rest of the oil in a pan. Fry the balls until golden.
10. Place the balls to drain on a plate with kitchen paper. Serve.

Spinach & Potato Croquettes

Eggs with Tuna Fish

1 onion

1 clove of garlic

1 carrot

1 kg tomatoes

6 tablesp. olive oil

Salt

Pepper

1 teasp. sugar

150 g tuna fish in pickled sauce

4 eggs

Fried bread

METHOD FOR 4 PORTIONS

1. Peel and finely chop the onion, garlic and carrot.
2. Scald the tomatoes in boiling water for 2 minutes so that they will be easier to peel. Remove skin and chop.
3. Heat the oil in a pan and sauté the above ingredients. Season with salt and pepper.
4. Strain the sauce. Check seasoning and add a little sugar to balance the acidity of the tomatoes.
5. Crumble the tuna fish and add it to the tomato sauce. Stir well and pour into an oven dish.
6. Break the eggs over the top, taking care that the yolks don't break. Put into a preheated oven at 250°C. Cook until the egg whites have set.
7. Remove the dish from the oven. Serve garnished with slices of fried bread.

250 g Cabrales cheese (blue cheese)

1/2 litre milk

25 g Philadelphia cheese

1 tablesp. butter

3 tablesp. flour

2 eggs

Breadcrumbs

Olive oil

Salt

Cheese Bites

METHOD FOR 4 PORTIONS

1. Mix the cheeses, the milk and the salt into a creamy consistency with no lumps.
2. Melt the butter in a pan. Add the flour and stir well using a wooden spoon. Let the mixture brown slightly. Add the cheese mixture and the milk, stirring continuously.
3. Cook for 10-15 minutes. Set aside to cool.
4. Cut the cold mixture into portions. Coat with flour, egg and breadcrumbs.
5. Deep-fry the portions in hot oil until golden on both sides, in small batches so that the oil doesn't lose its temperature. Drain well on kitchen paper. Serve.

Stuffed Avocados

4 avocados

5 crab sticks

2 cans of tuna fish in olive oil

1/2 onion

30 g sweetcorn

Juice of 1 lemon

For cocktail sauce:

1 egg

Olive oil

1 lemon

3 tablesp. tomato ketchup

1 teasp. whisky or brandy

A few drops of orange juice

1 tablesp. milk or cream

Salt

METHOD FOR 4 PORTIONS

1. Crumble the crab sticks.
2. Drain the tuna and break it up into small pieces. Chop the onion finely.
3. Make a thick mayonnaise with the egg, the oil and the salt. Add the lemon juice, the ketchup, the whisky, the orange juice and the milk.
4. In a bowl, mix the crab, the tuna, the onion and the sweetcorn. Add the sauce and stir well.
5. Peel the avocados, cut in half lengthwise and remove the stones. Sprinkle immediately with lemon juice so that they don't turn black.
6. Using a teaspoon, fill each cavity with the fish mixture.
7. Chill in the refrigerator, covering them with cling film.

Stuffed Avocados

Ratatouille, La Mancha-Style

(Pisto manchego)

½ kg courgettes

½ kg ripe tomatoes

½ kg peppers

2 medium-sized onions

5 tablesp. olive oil

1 clove of garlic

Salt

1 teasp. sugar

METHOD FOR 4 PORTIONS

1. Peel the onion and the garlic and chop finely.
2. Wash and chop the parsley.
3. Wash the peppers, deseed and cut into not-too-small pieces.
4. Scald the tomatoes in boiling water for 2 minutes so as to make them easier to peel. Peel, deseed and chop up.
5. Peel and dice the courgettes.
6. Heat the oil in a pan and sauté the onion, the garlic and the parsley, stirring from time to time, until the onion is soft.
7. Add the peppers, cover and cook over a low heat.
8. Next add the courgettes and the tomatoes. Cover and cook over a low heat for 15 minutes until ready.
9. Check seasoning and, if necessary, add a teaspoonful of sugar to balance the acidity of the tomato.

Pisto manchego

Snails with Ham

1 kg snails

300 g salt

1 glass of vinegar

1 onion

2 cloves of garlic

1 sprig of parsley

100 g cured ham

Olive oil

Tomato sauce

1 bay leaf

Thyme

Clove

Pepper

METHOD FOR 4 PORTIONS

1. If possible, choose vine snails, in autumn. They must be very clean and must be starved for 10 days.
2. Using a sharp knife, scrape off any slime. Wash in a bowl with lukewarm water to remove any sand. Repeat the operation several times. Leave the snails in the bowl, add three handfuls of salt, the vinegar and lukewarm water. Soak for 2 hours, moving from time to time.
3. After 2 hours, add some more water. Scrub the snails and change the water until they are completely clean.
4. Put the snails in a pan with cold water. Leave them for a while until they come out of their shells. Boil for 10 minutes. Drain and set to one side.
5. Finely chop the onion, the garlic and the parsley.
6. Dice the ham.
7. Heat some oil in a frying pan. When hot, sauté the onion, the garlic and the parsley. Cook well. Add the ham, a little tomato sauce, the bay leaf, the thyme, some pepper and the clove. Season. When the sauce is ready, add the drained snails and stir a little. Cover with water and cook for 3 hours.

8 pastry rounds for making turnovers

3 eggs

1 can of tuna fish in olive oil

1 can of sweet red peppers

1/2 onion

1/2 kg ripe tomatoes

Olive oil

Salt

Tuna Turnovers

(Empanadillas de atún)

METHOD FOR 4 PORTIONS

1. Hard boil the eggs (10 minutes). Peel and chop.
2. Drain the tuna and break it up.
3. Drain the red pepper. Remove any seeds and chop it up like the eggs.
4. Wash the tomatoes. Scald them in boiling water for 2 minutes so that they will be easier to peel. Remove skin and chop finely, together with the onion.
5. Heat a little oil in a frying pan and sauté the tomatoes and onion. When the tomato is ready, add a little sugar to cut the acidity. Season.
6. Add the tuna fish, the pepper and the eggs to the tomato sauce. Mix well and leave to cool.
7. Roll out the pastry rounds and put a little of the filling in the centre of each.
8. Fold the pastry over, dampen the edges and press them together firmly with a fork so that the filling doesn't come out when frying.
9. Deep-fry until golden.

Garlic Mushrooms

(Champiñones al ajillo)

1 kg mushrooms

4 cloves of garlic

Parsley

1 lemon

5 tablesp. olive oil

Salt

METHOD FOR 4 PORTIONS

1. Mushrooms should not be cleaned under the tap; it is preferable to use a napkin to get rid of any sand. Cut into slices.
2. Squeeze the juice of 1 lemon and sprinkle it over the mushrooms to prevent them from turning black.
3. Peel the cloves of garlic and slice finely.
4. Heat the oil in a pan and sauté the garlic, stirring continuously so that it doesn't burn.
5. Season the mushrooms and add them to the pan together with the lemon juice. Cook for 5 minutes and, when just about ready, sprinkle with chopped parsley.
6. Serve piping hot.

Champiñones al ajillo

Ham & Veal Croquettes

50 g ham

125 g minced veal

½ litre milk

40 g lard

200 g breadcrumbs

1 egg

10 tablesp. flour

Salt

Pepper

Olive oil

METHOD FOR 4 PORTIONS

1. Melt the lard in a pan. Add the minced veal.
2. Finely dice the ham and add it to the pan with the mince.
3. When the meat is cooked, add the flour, stirring continuously whilst adding the cold milk, taking care that no lumps are formed. Cook for a good while.
4. Season, pour into a shallow dish and leave to cool.
5. It is best to leave the croquette dough for at least four hours at room temperature.
6. Put the filling into a piping bag with no nozzle and a wide opening. Fill a tray with breadcrumbs and pipe out the croquette dough. Cut the dough into equal-sized croquettes.
7. Beat 1 egg, 1 tablespoonful of flour and 3 tablespoonfuls of water in a bowl. Using 2 forks, coat each croquette in the egg and then in the breadcrumbs.
8. Deep-fry in hot oil until golden. Remove from heat. Drain on kitchen paper.

Ham & Veal Croquettes

Sweet Tapas

Date

& Bacon Nibbles

8 dates

8 thin slices of bacon

8 almonds

Olive oil

METHOD FOR 4 PORTIONS

1. Stone the dates and fill each one with an almond. Be careful not to break the date.
2. Cut the bacon slices into the same size as the dates.
3. Wrap bacon round each date and secure with a cocktail stick.
4. Place the date rolls on a baking tray.
5. Preheat the oven to 250°C and grill for approximately 3 minutes until the bacon is golden.
6. They can also be fried in a pan with hot oil, in small batches so that the oil doesn't lose its temperature. Watch they don't burn.
7. Serve piping hot.

Date & Bacon Nibbles

Apple Fritters

4 apples

Juice of 1 lemon

75 g sugar

Olive oil

Carbonated water

1 sachet of baking powder

METHOD FOR 4 PORTIONS

1. Peel and core the apples. Cut into slices of approximately 1/2 cm.
2. Put the apple slices into a bowl. Drizzle at once with the lemon juice so that they don't turn black. Add two spoonfuls of sugar and leave for 1 hour.
3. Pour the carbonated water into a bowl. Add the baking powder and the flour. Using a mixer, beat well into a fine batter.
4. Coat the apple slices in the batter.
5. Heat the oil in a pan. Fry the slices until golden, in small batches, taking care that they don't burn.
6. When golden, place the fritters to drain on kitchen paper.
7. Turn onto another dish and serve sprinkled with sugar.

Apple Fritters

San Marcos Cake

(Tarta de San Marcos)

200 g whipping cream

Sponge cake:

6 eggs

200 g sugar

400 g flour

1 sachet of baking powder

20 g butter

Salt

Chocolate cream:

200 g cooking chocolate

200 g whipped cream

Sugared yolk topping:

100 g sugar

Yolks of 8 eggs

METHOD FOR 4 PORTIONS

1. Separate the egg yolks from the whites. Whisk the whites with a pinch of salt until firm. Cream the yolks with the sugar, stirring continuously for 10 minutes. Sift the flour in, stirring all the time. Add the melted butter.
2. Grease a rectangular cake tin with butter and coat with flour. Put the mixture into the tin. Bake in a preheated oven at 220°C for 20 minutes.
3. When ready, take the cake out of the oven and leave it to cool.
4. Whip the cream and put it in the refrigerator.
5. Melt the chocolate. Mix it with the cream and keep in the refrigerator.
6. For the sugared yolk topping, mix the yolks with the sugar in a bowl. Pour into a pan and cook over a very low heat, stirring all the time with a wooden spoon, until it thickens. Remove from heat.
7. Cut the sponge cake into three layers with a sharp knife. Place one layer on a plate, spread with the chocolate cream. Cover with another layer of sponge cake. Top this with whipped cream, another layer of cake and, finally with the sugared yolk topping.

Tarta de San Marcos

Mini Cream Puffs

Olive oil

5 cl whipping cream

Icing sugar

Choux pastry:

12.5 cl water

A pinch of salt

25 g sugar

50 g butter

80 g flour

2 large eggs

METHOD FOR 4 PORTIONS

1. Put the water in a pan together with the salt, the sugar and the butter and bring to the boil. When it starts to boil, remove the pan from the heat and tip in the sifted flour all at once. Beat well with a wooden spoon. Return the dough to the heat, stirring all the time, until it is quite firm.

2. Turn the dough into a bowl. Beat the eggs and add them gradually, mixing well into a smooth dough.

3. Make small balls and fry them in hot oil until slightly golden in small batches. Put on kitchen paper to drain. Leave to cool. Set to one side.

4. Whip the cream. Before doing so make sure that the bowl, the utensils and the cream are very cold (put them in the fridge a while before).

5. Put the cream into a forcing bag. Fill the choux pastries with cream (previously slit open on one side).

6. Place the cream puffs on a serving dish and sprinkle with icing sugar.

Mini Cream Puffs

Mini Chocolate Custard Cream Puffs

Choux Pastry:

12.5 cl water

A pinch of salt

25 g sugar

50 g butter

80 g flour

2 large eggs

Chocolate Custard Filling:

1/2 litre milk

Yolks of 3 eggs

3 tablesp. corn flour

75 g sugar

25 g butter

Rind of 1 lemon

50 g cocoa powder

Fondant Topping:

125 g sugar

100 g butter

3 ounces of chocolate

4 tablesp. water

METHOD FOR 4 PORTIONS

1. Put the water in a pan together with the salt, the sugar and the butter and bring to the boil. When it starts to boil, remove the pan from the heat and tip in the sifted flour all at once. Beat well with a wooden spoon. Return the dough to the heat, stirring all the time, until it is quite firm.
2. Turn the dough into a bowl. Beat the eggs and add them gradually, mixing well into a smooth dough.
3. Make strips of dough, and place them on a baking sheet. Bake in a preheated oven at 220°C for 35 minutes. Leave to cool. Set to one side.
4. Make the custard filling by putting the yolks, sugar and corn flour into a pan and gradually pouring in the milk (previously boiled). Stir well.
5. Add the lemon rind. Beat the mixture and bring to the boil, stirring all the time. When it starts to boil, remove from the heat. Add the butter and the cocoa and stir. Put the custard filling into a forcing bag and leave to cool.
6. Slit the choux pastries lengthwise. Fill with the chocolate custard.
7. Make the fondant by heating the water and sugar in a pan to make a syrup. Next, melt the chocolate in another pan and then add the syrup. When lukewarm, add the butter whilst beating. Finally, coat each choux pastry with fondant and leave to cool.

Mini Chocolate Custard Cream Puffs

Mini Custard Cream Tarts

Pastry:

60 g hazelnuts

60 g walnuts

120 g butter

120 g flour

60 g sugar

Custard Filling:

½ litre milk

100 g sugar

Yolks of 6 eggs

50 g flour

Stick of cinnamon

1 lemon

Yolk Topping:

½ litre water

200 g sugar

Yolks of 4 eggs

METHOD FOR 4 PORTIONS

1. Finely chop the hazelnuts and walnuts. Set to one side.
2. Put the butter into a bowl. Rub in the flour with your fingertips until it resembles a breadcrumb consistency. Add the sugar, the chopped nuts and knead into a smooth dough.
3. Make balls. Roll them out with a rolling pin. Grease small tart tins and line them with the pastry dough. Bake in a preheated oven at 190°C for 20 minutes.
4. Meanwhile, prepare the custard filling. Put the milk in a pan with the cinnamon stick. Bring to the boil, remove the pan from heat and put to one side to cool.
5. Beat the yolks and the sugar in a bowl. Mix well. Add the flour dissolved in a little cold milk. Mix with the boiled milk and the lemon rind.
6. Cook over a low heat until the pastry cream thickens, being careful that it doesn't boil. Leave to cool. Put the pastry cream into a forcing bag and fill the tarts.
7. Meanwhile, put the water and the sugar in a pan. Bring to the boil and add the yolks to this syrup. Remove from the heat and leave to stand for 5 minutes. Take the yolk topping out of the pan and leave to cool.
8. Carefully spoon a little of the yolk topping onto each tart. Sprinkle with a dash of cinnamon.

Mini Custard Cream Tarts

Original title in Spanish: *Tapas*

Translated by: Carole Patton

Project Editor: Isabel Ortiz

Edition: Working Image & Design S.L.

Managing Editor: Concha López

Production Controller: Antonia Mª Martínez

Photography: Concha López

Styling: Laura García

Layout: Lufercomp S.L.

Pre-printing: Miguel Ángel San Andrés

Digital imaging: José de Haro

Distribution: Carlos Nafarrate

Our most sincere thanks to Jesús Vega for his help in making and garnishing the dishes, as well as to the shop Casa for providing the tableware.

Campezo, 13 - 28022 Madrid
Tel.: 91 3009100 - Fax: 91 3009118
Impreso y encuadernado en España
www.susaeta.com

D.L.: M-36990-MMXV